HOMESTYLE
JAPANESE COOKING
IN PICTURES

HOMESTYLE JAPANESE COOKING
IN PICTURES

Sadako Kohno

Tempura
天ぷら (*Tempura*)
(*See page 26*)

SHUFUNOTOMO/JAPAN PUBLICATIONS

© Copyright in Japan 1977 by Sadako Kohno
Illustrations by Bunji Yoshinaga

Paper Over Board Edition
First printing: September 1991

Published by SHUFUNOTOMO CO., LTD.
2-9, Kanda Surugadai, Chiyoda-ku, Tokyo, 101 Japan

Sole Overseas Distributor: Japan Publications Trading CO., LTD.
P.O. Box 5030 Tokyo International, Tokyo, Japan
Distributors:
UNITED STATES: Kodansha America, Inc., through Farrar, Straus &
Giroux, 19 Union Square West, New York, NY 10003.
CANADA: Fitzhenry & Whiteside Ltd., 195 Allstate Parkway, Markham,
Ontario L3R 4T8.
BRITISH ISLES AND EUROPEAN CONTINENT: Premier Book Marketing Ltd.,
1 Gower Street, London WC1E 6HA.
AUSTRALIA AND NEW ZEALAND: Bookwise International,
54 Crittenden Road, Findon, South Australia 5023.
THE FAR EAST AND JAPAN: Japan Publications Trading Co., Ltd.,
1-2-1, Sarugaku-cho, Chiyoda-ku, Tokyo 101.

ISBN 0-87040-423-7
Printed in Japan

Preface

Every country of the world has tasty food characteristic of its cultural background, climate, and resources. Japan is no exception. The change of seasons in Japan is very distinct, and as a result we have a variety of food, differing according to the four seasons. In addition, we are surrounded by the ocean which provides us with an abundance of seafood. The atmosphere of the cuisine being as important as the taste, the Japanese people have also put their hearts and souls into the arrangement of the food, emphasizing the fragrance and characteristics of the different seasons, thus making the dishes, I believe, works of art which we can very well be proud of.

As more and more people visit Japan and have the opportunity to taste Japanese food, it is gaining favor among people of other countries as well. They are attracted by both the beauty and the taste. Moreover, since Japanese food is not only comparatively low in calories, but also nutritious because of the skillful use of vegetable protein, its value has been recognized among those who are conscious of their health.

I have been interested in cooking since I was 20 and have studied the art of cooking in various ways until this my 78th year of age. When I was young, I lived in New York for 12 years as my husband worked for the Mitsui Co. there. During our stay in New York, I experimented with ways to make palatable Japanese dishes using materials available at the local shops.

After my return to Japan, I rediscovered the value of Japanese food. On the one hand, I have taken every opportunity possible to continue studying the art of cooking, and on the other hand I have tried to spread knowledge of Japanese cookery for the home by teaching foreigners living in Japan, publishing books on cooking, and giving demonstrations on T. V.

Today it is easier to acquire the necessary ingredients and seasoning for Japanese cooking abroad, and consequently easier to make Japanese food. Making use of my many years of experience in this field, I have selected dishes that have proven universally popular and have also tried to suggest substitutes for materials which may be difficult to obtain.

I should be very happy if this book is of help to those who wish to try to make Japanese food themselves.

Sadako Kohno

Sadako Kohno
Tokyo, Japan

Contents

Each recipe is for 4 servings.

6

Kitchen Utensils

Bamboo chopsticks

Sudare (bamboo mat or screen)

Steamer

Wooden spatula

Deba-bocho (boning knife for fish)

Usuba-bocho (cutting knife for vegetables)

Tamago pan (a rectangular Japanese egg pan)

Grater

Hand strainer

Suribachi (serrated mixing bowl) and wooden pestle

Cooking chopsticks

Sieve

Tableware for Japanese Dishes

Chopsticks

Individual serving dishes (small)

Soy pot

Sauceboat

Tea cups

Teapot

Bowl for *nimono*

Plate for *yakimono*

Rice bowl

Soup bowl

Porcelain spoon

Chawan-mushi bowl

5 wide plates

Platter and 5 medium plates

Sakazuki (wine cup)

Tokkuri (liquor bottle)

Bowl for pickles

Individual serving bowls

Do-nabe (earthernware casserole)

Cutting and Slicing — The Japanese Way

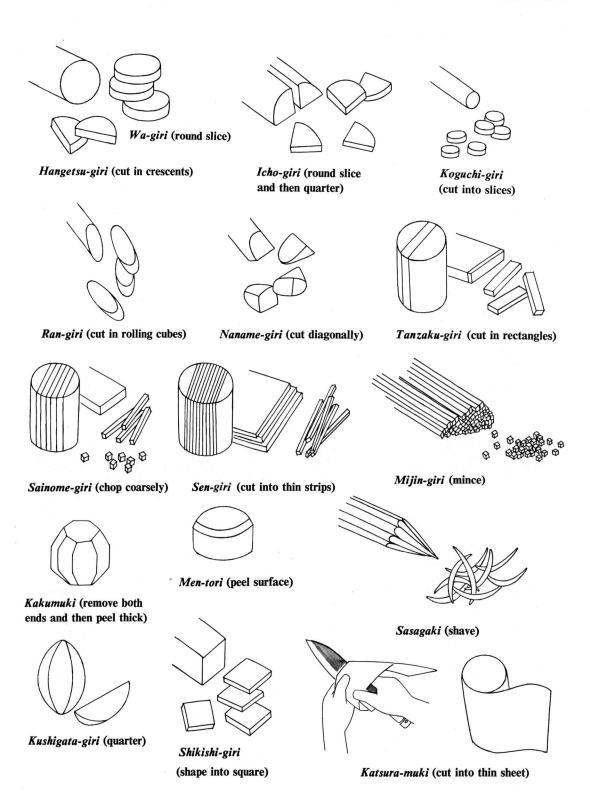

Wa-giri (round slice)

Hangetsu-giri (cut in crescents)

Icho-giri (round slice and then quarter)

Koguchi-giri (cut into slices)

Ran-giri (cut in rolling cubes)

Naname-giri (cut diagonally)

Tanzaku-giri (cut in rectangles)

Sainome-giri (chop coarsely)

Sen-giri (cut into thin strips)

Mijin-giri (mince)

Kakumuki (remove both ends and then peel thick)

Men-tori (peel surface)

Sasagaki (shave)

Kushigata-giri (quarter)

Shikishi-giri (shape into square)

Katsura-muki (cut into thin sheet)

Artistic Cutting

Crisscross mushroom caps

How to tie *mitsuba*

How to cut *yuzu*, lemon rind

round

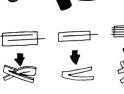

pine leaves   **strips**

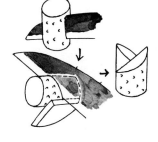

Cucumber rings

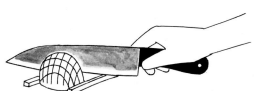

Kikka-kabu (cut like chrysanthemum flowers)

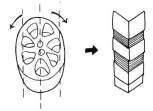

Arrow-shaped lotus root

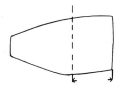

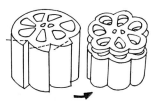

Flower-shaped lotus root

11

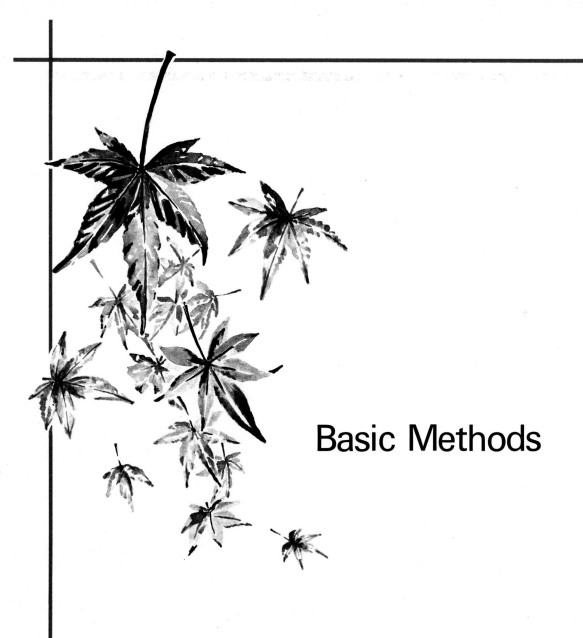

Basic Methods

Egg Drop Soup (*Kakitama-jiru*)

かき玉汁

Ingredients:

2 eggs, beaten
1 tablespoon *sake*
a dash of salt
4 cups *dashi* (bonito soup), see page 65
1⅓ teaspoons salt
1 teaspoon soy sauce
2 teaspoons cornstarch, dissolved in 2 tablespoons cold water
6 stalks *mitsuba* (trefoil), cut into 1″ lengths, or parboiled spinach leaves
kinomé leaves for garnish (optional)

Method:

1. Beat eggs in bowl; add 1 tablespoon *sake*, a dash of salt; mix thoroughly   **(1)**
2. Add 1⅓ teaspoons salt to *dashi*; cook over medium heat. Bring to a boil. Season with 1 teaspoon soy sauce.
3. Pour cornstarch over boiling soup; cook until thickened.   **(2)**
4. Stir soup with chopsticks to avoid overboiling. Gradually add egg mixture, stirring constantly.
5. Bring to a boil; add *mitsuba*; turn off heat immediately. Pour into individual soup bowls; garnish with *kinomé*.   **(3)**

Tamago-toji—For Spring

Hagi Tamago—For Fall

Sugomori Tamago—For Summer

Miso Soup with *Tofu* and *Wakame* (*Misoshiru*)

とうふとわかめのみそ汁

Ingredients:

4 cups *niboshi-dashi* (dried fish soup)
2 oz. *wakamé*, washed, drained and cut into 1″ length pieces
3 tablespoons *aka* (dark) *miso*
1–1½ tablespoons *shiro* (white) *miso*
1 square *tofu*
½ green onion, chopped

Method:

1. Use *niboshi-dashi* for soup. See page 66 for directions.
2. Soften *wakamé* in water. Remove hard parts; cut in 1″ lengths.
3. Place *miso* in small strainer or in bowl; add *dashi*, dissolve by pressing with back of ladle; add to boiling *dashi*.   **(1)**
4. Taste: Taste should be a little stronger than desired because *tofu* and *wakamé* will be added later.
5. Add *wakamé*; heat 1–2 minutes.
6. Remove *tofu* from water; cut into halves; place one half at a time on palm, cut into ½″ cubes, letting them drop into soup as they are cut. Be careful not to overboil soup after *miso* is added.   **(2–3)**
7. When *tofu* is heated and begins to float to surface, add chopped green onion; turn off heat; pour into bowls. Serve hot.   **(4)**

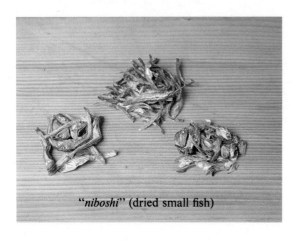

"*niboshi*" (dried small fish)

miso paste

Sliced Raw Fish (*Sashimi*)

さしみ

Ingredients:
½–1 lb. raw fish fillet
Sashimi no Tsuma, see photograph
wasabi powder

To Cut *Sashimi*:
1. *Sogi-Zukuri*: Slant knife, and slice from right to left. Lift slice toward your left, and lay each slice one on top of the other to the right. **(1)**
2. *Hiki-Zukuri*: Cut straight down, then pull knife towards you. Do not saw back and forth. **(2)**

Sashimi no Tsuma (Garnishing for sliced raw fish):
Garnishing may be any thinly shredded raw vegetable that gives a fresh, crisp appearence. The most common are *daikon*, cabbage, cucumber, carrot, *shiso* leaves, leeks or green onions. Soak in water and drain. Flowered radishes may also be used.

To Serve:
Garnishing is important with *sashimi*. The little greenish mound is *wasabi* (Japanese horseradish). It comes in powdered form and is mixed with a few drops of water. Each person should be given a small dish of soy sauce into which he mixes *wasabi* to taste. The pieces of *sashimi* are dipped into the sauce before eating.

Tsuma of *Sashimi*

myoga cucumber *shiraga-daikon* carrot cabbage

murame *ao-jiso* *akame* *yori-udo* *yori*-cucumber

seaweed seaweed seaweed red-*nori* *ao-jiso* leaf

hana-ho-jiso

bofu radishes and cucumbers *ho-jiso*

19

Rainbow Trout Grilled with Salt (*Nijimasu no Shioyaki*)

にじますの塩焼き

Ingredients:
4 rainbow trout
salt
4 Vinegared Fresh Ginger, see page 91

Preparation:
Rub fish lightly with salt. Pull out gills and scale from tail side upward to head. Make a 2″ slit near pectoral fin; remove entrails. Clean and wash. Drain.

To Salt: Fish are salted not only for seasoning but to remove the fishy odor. The proper amount of salt is 2–3% of the weight of the fish. Sprinkle salt evenly on both sides of fish. Let stand about 10 minutes until salt sets.   **(1)**

To Skewer: Insert skewer near eye of fish along center line, trying not to let skewer pierce through other side. Thread by bringing skewer back up toward you and then down again into center of fish. With head of skewer move up and down inside of fish toward tail. Finally, bring skewer up near tail. This makes the tail stand up, when cooked.
   Insert another skewer near mouth and pierce through fish in the same pattern as first skewer to secure fish while cooking. The two skewers should slightly spread near tail.   **(2)**

Kesho-jio: Press surface of fish with towel to dry. Spread all fins; rub fins with a generous amount of salt till all fins become completely white. Sprinkle fish with salt again. Called "*kesho-jio*," this salting prevents fins from burning and breaking off when broiled. Wrapping fins in foil is recommended to prevent them from burning.   **(3)**

To Serve: Arrange fish on an oblong dish with head on your left. It looks prettier to place fish diagonally with tail standing. Garnish with vinegared fresh ginger, slanted against side of fish. Trim with bamboo leaves or some green leaves, if desired. Serve immediately, and sprinkle with choice of lemon juice, soy sauce or ginger juice.

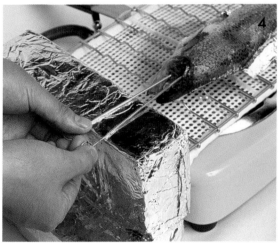

To Broil: Place gridiron over high heat. When gridiron is thoroughly heated, place fish with head facing right **(4)**. When nicely browned, twist skewers to prevent them from sticking. Lower heat, turn over fish and broil slowly till firm in center, about 12–15 minutes. Turn only once. If turned several times, skin will peel and meat will break off. For finishing touch, brown as in picture. This is to finish broiling and to eliminate the fishy odor. Place on cutting **(5-6)**

Chicken *Teriyaki* (*Tori no Teriyaki*)

鶏のなべ照り焼き

Ingredients:
2–3 chicken thighs, boned
Marinade A:
   3 tablespoons soy sauce
   1 tablespoon *sake* or dry sherry
   1 tablespoon *mirin*
   1 teaspoon fresh ginger juice
3 tablespoons salad oil
Mixture B:
   1 tablespoon *mirin*
   1 tablespoon sugar
Sansho powder
Ashirai (garnish):
   Turnip Flowers, see page 91

Method:
1. Pierce chicken through skin to marinade thoroughly and to prevent from shrinking when cooked. Mix Marinade A and marinate chicken for 20–30 minutes. **(1)**
2. Heat 3 tablespoons salad oil in frying pan; shake off excess liquid from chicken; sauté—skin side down, over medium heat. **(2)**
3. When browned, turn. Reduce heat, cook covered—about 10 minutes.
4. Remove chicken from pan, drain, pour remaining marinade into pan. Add Mixture B; bring to a boil.
5. Add chicken again. Cook until marinade is almost cooked away.
6. Remove chicken from pan, sprinkle with powdered *sansho*. Slice in ½″ ¾″ diagonally. Garnish with Turnip Flowers or green peppers sautéed in pan.

Ashirai, see pages 11, 93

Vinegared lotus roots

Kikka-kabu

Fried chili pepper

Vinegared radishes   Glazed Black Beans

Pickled plums

Glazed orange peel

cucumber

Udo

Flower-shaped radishes   Pickled *myoga*   Pickled onions   Sweet vinegared ginger

Rolled Omelet (*Dashimaki Tamago*)

Ingredients:
6 eggs, beaten
Mixture A:
   6–8 tablespoons *dashi* (bonito soup)
   ½ teaspoon salt
   1 teaspoon light soy sauce
   1 teaspoon *mirin* or *sake*
   1 tablespoon sugar
2 tablespoons salad oil
Garnishes: toasted black sesame seeds (optional)
6 tablespoons grated *daikon* mixed with a few drops of soy sauce
Sweet Vinegared Ginger, see page 91

Method:
1. Break eggs in bowl, beat thoroughly; add Mixture A.
2. Heat skillet over medium heat. Add 2 tablespoons salad oil, tilt skillet so bottom and side are well greased. Drain off excess oil. Slightly wipe skillet with paper towel.
3. Drop small amount of egg mixture with chopsticks into pan to test. When hot enough to sizzle, pour in ½ of egg mixture, tilt skillet to spread mixture evenly. When it starts bubbling and begins to set, roll up toward yourself with chopsticks; leave in pan. **(1)**
4. Grease rest of skillet thoroughly with oiled paper. Slide rolled egg toward opposite side, grease space.
5. Pour in half of remaining mixture, lift up rolled egg, letting mixture flow underneath to cover the whole bottom of skillet. When this egg begins to set, again bring the whole egg roll toward you. Repeat the process with remaining egg mixture. **(2–4)**
6. Remove from skillet. Place on bamboo screen or dry cloth. Roll up while still hot. Press gently to form good shape. Let it stand about 15 minutes. **(5–6)**
7. When cooled, cut into 1″–1½″ slices.
8. Arrange 2 or 3 slices on each plate with cut sides up. Sprinkle with a few black sesame seeds on top, if desired. Garnish with grated *daikon* and sweet vinegared ginger.

Tempura (*Tempura*)

天ぷら

Ingredients and Kitchen Preparation:

12 shrimp; devein and shell, leaving heads and tails on. Cut off tips of tails, push out water from tails with back of knife. So shrimp will not curl up when fried, make a few cuts on inside curve. Stretch to straighten.

4 *kisu* or any small fish with white meat; cut off heads, cut open and spread out. Remove backbone and entrails.

1 cuttlefish; pull out entrails. Remove skin. Cut into rectangles. Make cuts on sides to prevent shrinking.

12 green peppers; skewer three peppers on each toothpick.

4 fresh *shiitake;* cut off stems.

4 young fresh ginger roots; cut leaves off. Clean roots.

Batter:
  1 egg
  ½ cup cold water
  1 cup flour
oil for deep-frying

Tentsuyu Sauce: See page 90
  1 cup *dashi* (bonito soup), see page 65
  ¼–⅓ cup soy sauce
  ¼–⅓ cup *mirin*

Momiji-Oroshi, see pages **38**, 82

To Make Batter: (For light batter, use sifted flour and ice-cold water.)

Beat egg; stir in water. Add flour, mix lightly with chopsticks, using thick ends. Do not place batter near fire nor leave it too long before using, as it will become gluey. Only make one batch of batter at a time.

To Fry:

1. Fill a deep-frying pan with frying oil to about 1″ from top. The oil should be at least 3″ deep. Start heating oil when you begin to make batter. Bring to medium heat when batter is ready.
2. Test the temperature by dropping small amount of batter into oil with chopsticks.
3. Do not try to fry too much at a time. No more than half the surface of oil should be covered. Turn only once. When crisp, remove from oil, shake once or twice above oil to take off excess oil.
4. Drain on rack or on paper towels arranged on baking pan or in colander. Do not lay one on top of another or else they will get soggy.
5. Skim off excess droppings from oil before frying a new batch.
6. When oil temperature reaches 320°F. begin frying green peppers.

(Continned on page 28)

Vegetable *Tempura* (*Shojin-age*)

精進揚げ

Ingredients:

1 small sweet potato or potato
1 piece lotus root (3″ long)
4 eggplants
1 carrot (2″ long)
1 piece *dashi kombu* (8″ long), cut into 2″ × ½″
  pieces
20 slender string beans
20 *sōmen* (thin noodles)
8 dried *nori*, cut into ½″ strips

4 stalks young, fresh ginger root
4 fresh *shiitake*
Batter:
  1 egg
  ⅔ cup cold water
  1 cup sifted flour
2 teaspoons grated fresh ginger
Tentsuyu Sauce: See "Tempura" recipe
grated *daikon* mixed with grated fresh ginger

Method:

1. Pare sweet potato and lotus root. Cut into ½″ round slices. Soak both in water in separate bowls about 10 minutes.
2. Trim eggplant as in picture. Cut into halves lengthwise. Again cut lengthwise into thin strips to within ½″ of top.
3. Cut carrot ⅛″ thick. Then slice in the same manner as egglpant, leaving ¼″ intact at one end.
4. Put two pieces of *kombu* together, make a ½″ cut in center, pull one end through hole, so it will look like a tied ribbon.
5. String the beans. Tie 5 together with strips of *nori*. Use batter for paste. Break noodles into halves. Roll *nori* around one end of a bunch of about 10 noodles, paste *nori* together with batter.
6. Prepare ginger and *shiitake* as in former "Tempura" recipe.
7. Beat egg lightly, add enough water to make ¾ cup of liquid. Mix in a little more than 1 cup sifted flour. Make batter a little thicker than Tempura batter. Add 2 teaspoons grated fresh ginger to flavor, if desired.
8. To fry string beans: Dip only ends into batter. As for eggplants and carrots, spread out cut sides, dip in batter. Fry noodles without dipping in batter. Other ingredients (ginger root, *shiitake*) are fried as in former "Tempura" recipe.

(*Continued from page 26*)

7. When oil is heated to about 340°F. fry ginger, dipping only root part in batter. Dip bottom side of *shiitake* in batter. Fry on coated side first, turn.
8. When oil is heated to about 370°F. coat cuttlefish with flour and dip in batter. Slip gently into hot oil.
9. Hold tail end of shrimp, dip in batter, shake off excess batter. Slip into hot oil. Do the same with *kisu* (sillaginoid).

(1-2)

To Make *Tentsuyu* Sauce: See page 90
To Make *Momiji-Oroshi*:   See pages 38, 82

To Serve:

Place on white paper folded at an angle on plate. Serve with *Momiji-Oroshi* and *Tentsuyu* Sauce in small individual bowls.

Boiled Dried Bean Curd with Shrimp Balls (*Takiawase*)

えびだんごと高野どうふのたき合わせ

Ingredients:

3 pieces *koya-dofu* (dried frozen bean curd)
3–4 *kikurage* (cloud-ear mushrooms)
⅔ lb. shrimp
1 egg
Mixture A:
   2 tablespoons *sake* or dry sherry
   1 tablespoon cornstarch
   ½ teaspoon salt
½ lb. green beans; cook in boiling salt water
   until tender but crisp, drain and sprinkle
   with little salt and *mirin*.

2½ cups *dashi* (bonito soup)
Mixture B:
   3 tablespoons *mirin*
   3 tablespoons sugar
   1 tablespoon soy sauce
   1 teaspoon salt
Mixture C:
   1 tablespoon *mirin*
   salt and soy sauce to taste
a little *yuzu* rind, thinly shredded

Method:

1. Soften *koya-dofu* in hot water about 30 minutes. Drain. Place in cold water. Gently press with both hands under cold running water until water becomes clear. Drain; press out water; cut into squares of desired size. **(1–2)**
2. Soften *kikurage* in water about 10 minutes; cut into thin strips. Shell and devein shrimp, cut 3 oz. in small pieces. Grind remaining shrimp in *suribachi* or with blender. Slowly mix in lightly beaten egg. Add Mixture A; mix thoroughly. Add *kikurage* and small pieces of shrimp. **(4)**
3. Bring 3 cups water to a boil. Drop in shrimp mixture with tablespoon. When shrimp balls rise to surface, remove. Then simmer soup until reduced to about half. **(5)**
4. Bring to a boil 2½ cups *dashi* and Mixture B. Add *koya-dofu*. Place a smaller lid directly on top of *koya-dofu* before covering pan with its own lid. Bring to a boil; reduce heat; cook 20 minutes; cool. Add cooked string beans to pan for flavor. **(3)**
5. Add Mixture C to concentrated soup (4), add shrimp balls; simmer 10 minutes.

To Serve:

Arrange *koya-dofu*, shrimp balls, string beans on plate. Garnish with strips of *yuzu* rind, if desired.

3

4

5

6

Boiled Acorn Squash with Ground Beef (*Nimono*)

かぼちゃの煮物

Ingredients:

1 acorn squash (about 1 lb.)
2 pieces fresh ginger
Mixture A:
   2 tablespoons *sake* or dry sherry
   2 tablespoons sugar
   3 tablespoons soy sauce
½ lb. ground beef
Mixture B:
   1 tablespoon soy sauce
   1 tablespoon sugar
   2 teaspoons cornstarch, dissolved in 2–3 teaspoons cold water

Method:

1. Cut acorn squash in pieces about 1½″ in size. With spoon, scrape out seeds and stringy portion. Pare; round edges. **(1–2)**
2. Cut half of ginger in thin strips, soak in water to crisp. Chop remaining ginger.
3. In pan place chopped ginger and Mixture A. Heat; add ground beef, stir constantly with 5 or 6 chopsticks until liquid has almost cooked away. Place squash in pan, add Mixture B and water to cover. Place a smaller lid on top of squash before covering pan with its own cover. Bring to a boil. Reduce heat, simmer until tender. **(3–5)**
4. Remove squash, bring remaining mixture to a boil; stir in 2 teaspoons cornstarch and cook until thickened. **(6)**

To Serve:

Place squash on plate, spoon on ground meat, garnish with thinly cut ginger.

Steamed Egg Custard (*Chawanmushi*)

茶わん蒸し

Ingredients:

Dashi Mixture:
- 2¼–2½ cups *dashi* (bonito soup)
- ½ teaspoon salt
- 1 teaspoon *mirin*
- 1 teaspoon soy sauce
- 3 eggs, beaten
- 2 chicken breast, thinly sliced and sprinkled with ½ teaspoon soy sauce and 1 teaspoon

- *sake*
- 8 slices *kamaboko* (boiled fish cake). See sketch
- 12 ginkgo nuts, parboiled and skin removed
- 4 fresh *shiitake* caps, crisscrossed on top with knife. See sketch
- 8 shrimp, deveined, shelled except for tail; sprinkle with little salt and *sake*
- 8 stalks *mitsuba* (trefoil) or spinach.

Method:
1. Bring *Dashi* Mixture to a boil. Cool. Beat eggs lightly. Mix with cooled *dashi*. Pour mixture through fine strainer to ensure a smooth custard. Children often prefer a little more soy sauce and *mirin* added with less *dashi* for firmer custard. **(1)**
2. Place steam cooker with water over high heat.
3. Divide chicken, *kamaboko*, ginkgo nuts into 4 portions. Place in 4 individual serving cups or bowls. Pour egg mixture over all, filling each to about ½″ from top. Remove foam with spoon. Place *shiitake* on top, lay shrimp slightly over *shiitake*.
4. Without covering cups, place in hot steam cooker. The steamer lid should be wrapped in dish towel because water dropping from the lid will change taste and appearance of custard. Leave lid slightly ajar, to prevent temperature from rising too high. **(2)**
5. Reduce heat; steam 12 to 15 minutes. When almost set, garnish with trefoil. Insert toothpick in center of custard to test if custard is done. When soup comes out clear, it is ready to serve. Eat immediately with spoon. **(3)**

Note: Placing cups in a pot with hot water is an alternative if no steamer is available.

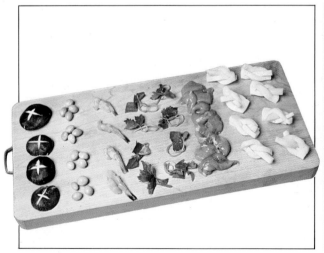

Sukiyaki (*Sukiyaki*)

すき焼き

Ingredients and Kitchen Preparation:

1–1½ lb. tender sirloin beef, sliced thinly, then cut into 4″ lengths

2 oz. beef fat

1 *shirataki*, parboiled, drained and cut into 2″ lengths

4 leeks (or green onion, spring onion), sliced diagonally (about 2″)

1 bunch *shungiku*; remove roots and cut into easily managed lengths

4–8 fresh *shiitake* caps, crisscrossed on top with knife

1 block *tofu*, cut into 1″ cubes, preferably *yaki-dofu* (roasted *tofu*)

yaki-fu, soaked in water and drained

4–6 raw eggs

Sukiyaki Sauce:

1 cup *kombu-dashi* (kelp soup)

½ cup soy sauce

½ cup *mirin*

3 tablespoons sugar

Table cooking:

1. Arrange meat and vegetables attractively on large platter.
2. Boil ½ cup *kombu-dashi* with other ingredients for Sukiyaki Sauce. The remaining *dashi* is placed in a suitable vessel to take to table.
3. On table place a grill, large platter with all ingredients, raw eggs, Sukiyaki Sauce, *kombu-dashi*, serving dishes, and pepper, if desired.
4. Preheat large skillet on high heat; add suet; rub over bottom to grease. Add portions of green onion and beef. Pour just enough Sukiyaki Sauce over beef to cover. Turn beef over a few times with cooking chopsticks. Add portions of vegetables and other ingredients, keeping them in separate groups. **(1–2)**
5. Serve and eat while cooking or let guests help themselves. In individual serving bowls beat lightly one egg for each guest. Use as a dip.
6. Add more ingredients and Sukiyaki Sauce as food is eaten. Do not overcook. When sauce has diminished, add *kombu-dashi* or Sukiyaki Sauce as desired. When there is too much liquid, add *yaki-fu* to absorb it.
7. After all ingredients have been eaten, pour in *kombu-dashi* or water, bring to a boil. Add cooked noodles or rice, if desired.

Chicken *Mizutaki* (*Mizutaki*)

水たき

Ingredients and Kitchen Preparation:

2½ lb. chicken thighs and breasts, chopped with bones into several pieces, washed and drained. Pass through boiling water. Bring 20 cups water, chicken, and 2 tablespoons washed rice (wrapped in gauze) to a boil over high heat. Lower heat and simmer, removing scum as it forms. Let chicken simmer about 60–90 minutes; remove and place on platter. Strain broth. Reserve.

1 *daikon* (4″ long) pared and cut into ⅓″ rings

Cabbage Rolls: Parboil 4 Chinese cabbage leaves and ½ bunch *shungiku* or spinach. Make a layer of cabbage on bamboo mat or thick cloth, and place *shungiku* on top. Roll up lightly squeezing out excess liquid, and cut into 1½″ lengths.

8 fresh *shiitake* caps, crisscrossed on top with knife

12 ginkgo nuts, boiled, skinned

½ carrot, sliced ⅕″ thick and cut in floral shapes

1 bunch *shirataki*, parboiled and drained. Cut into 2″ lengths.

½ bunch *mitsuba*, cut in halves

salt and MSG

Ponzu Sauce and Relishes:

Sarashi-negi: Shred green onion finely. Soak in water; drain; wrap in cloth; rub and wash well; wring out.

Momiji-Oroshi: With chopstick make several holes in cut end of pared *daikon*. Seed dried red pepper; cap onto pointed end of chopstick; insert in holes; remove chopstick; grate.

Yuzu rind: Cut rind into very thin strips

Ponzu Sauce: See page 90

Table Cooking:

1. Place cooked tender chicken in earthenware casserole. Fill casserole ¾ full with strained broth. Leave remaining broth for later use.
2. Arrange all ingredients; *daikon*, cabbage rolls, *shiitake* ginkgo nuts, carrot, *shirataki* attractively on large platter.
3. Place casserole on portable table cooker or *hibachi* on table. Set table with all ingredients, relishes, *Ponzu* Sauce, salt, MSG, and serving dishes.
4. Heat casserole over medium heat, add vegetables one after the other. Serve cooked portions or let guests help themselves.
5. Let guests choose their favorite relishes, dip in *Ponzu* Sauce.
6. When all has been eaten, add a few drops or soy sauce to broth, then boiled noodles or cooked rice, if desired.

38

Rice with Vegetables (*Gomoku Gohan*)

五目ごはん

Ingredients:

3½ oz. chicken breasts, cut into small pieces
1 teaspoon minced fresh ginger
2 tablespoons *sake* or dry sherry
2 tablespoons soy sauce
1 tablespoon sugar
½ block *konnyaku*, cut into ⅕″ strips
1 teaspoon soy sauce
3 cups raw rice
3 cups *dashi* (bonito soup)
1 tablespoon soy sauce

3 dried *shiitake* soaked in warm water for 20 minutes, drained and cut into thin strips
1 burdock root, peeled and cut in "*sasagaki*" (bamboo leaf) method; soak in cold water for 20 minutes, and drain
1 piece *abura-age;* pass through boiling water, cut in half and then cut into ⅕″ strips
½ carrot, peeled, cut into 1″ × ⅕″ size slices.
1 tablespoon minced parsley

Method:

1. Bring to a boil soy sauce, *sake*, sugar, ginger; add chicken. After cooking, drain chicken. Reserve liquid. **(1)**
2. Boil *konnyaku* strips; drain. Heat 1 teaspoon soy sauce in pan; add *konnyaku*; stir to coat with soy sauce.
3. Wash rice 1 hour ahead of cooking. Drain in colander. Set aside, cover with a damp dish towel.
4. Add enough *dashi* to liquid reserved from cooking chicken to make 3¼ cups liquid.
5. Place rice, 3¼ cups liquid, 1 tablespoon soy sauce, and all ingredients, except parsley, in heavy pan. Stir from bottom of pan, cover. Cook over high heat until it comes to a boil. Lower heat, cook about 12 minutes. Turn off heat. (As rice cooked with soy sauce tends to burn easily and takes longer time to absorb water, heat should be a little lower than when cooking plain rice, thus requiring more cooking time than usual.) **(2)**
6. Let it stand 15 minutes. With wooden spatula or fork, fluff up rice. Stir in 1 tablespoon minced parsley just before serving. **(3)**

Chestnut Rice,
see page 71

Rice with Green Peas,
see page 71

2

3

Vinegared Rice Rolled in *Nori* (*Nori-maki*)

Ingredients:

20 strips *kampyo* (7″ long)
Mixture A:
　3 tablespoons sugar
　3 tablespoons soy sauce
2 oz. halibut or white meat fish
Mixture B:
　¼ teaspoon salt
　1½ tablespoons sugar
　1½ tablespoons *sake*
　red food coloring
2 eggs
Mixture C:
　3 tablespoons *dashi* (bonito soup)

¼ teaspoon salt
2 tablespoons sugar
1 carrot, cut into 1¼″ length strips
Mxture D:
　a pinch of salt
　1 teaspoon sugar
3 *shiitake*, stemmed and softened in water
Mixture E:
　1½ tablespooons sugar
　1½ tablespoons soy sauce
　1 tablespoon *mirin*
16 stalks *mitsuba;* pass through boiling water
　and drain. Sprinkle with salt and MSG to taste.

Preparation:

1. *Kampyo:* Sprinkle *kampyo* with salt; wash. Soak *kampyo* in enough water to cover for at least 1 hour. Cook until tender; add Mixture A. Cook until liquid has almost cooked away. Cool.
2. Halibut (or some other white meat fish): Cook fish in boiling water; skin and bone. Wrap in damp cheesecloth, crumble fish into fine flakes. In small saucepan add Mixture B. Add fish flakes, stir with 5 or 6 chopsticks over low heat. If the flakes start to stick to bottom of pan, remove from heat and scrape off. Stir over low heat again, until fish becomes dry.
3. Eggs: Beat and mix in Mixture C. Fry in skillet and roll up as in "*Dashimaki Tamago*" (page 22). Cool. Cut into ½″ square sticks.
4. Carrot: Place carrot in pan, add Mixture D and water to cover. Cook until liquid has almost cooked away.
5. *Shiitake:* Place *shiitake* in pan, add Mixture E and water to cover. Cook until tender.

(Continued on page 86)

Udon with Chicken (*Nikomi Udon*)

煮込みうどん

Ingredients:

⅔ lb. dried *udon*

6½ cups *dashi* (bonito soup)

2–3 tablespoons *mirin*

6 tablespoons light soy sauce

a little salt

½ lb. chicken, sliced. Soak in 1 teaspoon soy sauce and 1 teaspoon *sake*.

4 fresh *shiitake* caps, crisscrossed on top with knife

1 green onion, cut into diagonal pieces

4 stalks spinach, parboiled in boiling water with 1 teaspoon sugar. Rinse in cold water and drain. Cut into 1″ lengths.

12 pieces carrot, cut in flower shapes and parboiled

4 eggs

1 sheet dried *nori*, if desired

1 tablespoon chopped green onion

7 flavor spices for seasoning

Method:

1. Bring to a boil generous amount of water in large kettle, add *udon* noodles. Boil, uncovered, stirring with chopsticks or fork. When it comes to a boil, add 1 cup water. When it comes to boiling point again, turn off heat. Cover. Let stand 10 minutes, or until as tender as spaghetti; drain into colander. Rinse in cold water; drain again. Set aside.   **(1–3)**
2. Add *mirin*, soy sauce, and salt to *dashi*. Bring to a boil.
3. Dip *udon* from colander into boiling water to warm. Drain. Place *udon* in large casserole (or in 4 small individual casseroles); add *dashi* (2); top with chicken, *shiitake*, green onion; cover. Cook over high heat. When it comes to a boil, add spinach and carrot. Break eggs into center of casserole; cover. Cook until eggs are of desired firmness. Turn off heat. Serve with finely chopped green onion and thin strips of *nori*.   **(4–6)**

Cucumber and Seaweed Salad (*Sunomono*)

きゅうりとわかめの酢の物

Ingredients:
3 tablespoons *shirasuboshi* (small dried fish)
Sambai-zu Dressing:
   3 tablespoons vinegar
   1 tablespoon soy sauce
   1 tablespoon sugar
   ½ teaspoon salt
   1 tablespoon water
3½ oz. *wakamé* (seaweed)
   ½ teaspoon vinegar
2 cucumbers
   1 teaspoon salt
   1 teaspoon vinegar
1 fresh ginger root

Method:
1. Clean *shirasuboshi;* wash; drain. Place in large bowl; add *Sambai-zu* Dressing.
2. Soften *wakamé* in water; discard hard parts; pour boiling water over *wakamé* immediately, soak in cold water to preserve bright color. Drain; cut into 1″ lengths; spread on colander, sprinkle with ½ teaspoon vinegar to flavor. **(1)**
3. Wash cucumbers; rub in salt by rolling on cutting board. Wash; cut off ends; slice thinly crosswise. **(2)**
4. Place slices into bowl; sprinkle with 1 teaspoon salt; rub lightly. Wash; drain; sprinkle with vinegar. **(3–4)**
5. Cut ginger into very thin strips.
6. Add cucumber, *wakamé* to *shirasuboshi*, mix lightly. **(5)**
7. Serve in small bowls; top with ginger strips.

 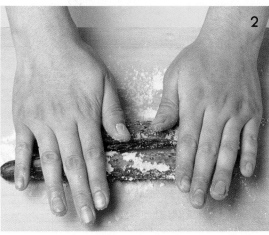

Egg Cake (*Nishiki Tamago*)

二色卵

Ingredients:
10 hard-boiled eggs
Mixture A:
  2 tablespoons sugar
  a pinch of salt
  ½ teaspoon *katakuriko* or conrnstarch
Mixture B:
  3 tablespoons sugar
  a pinch of salt
5 *kinomé* leaves for garnish

Method:
1. Mash hard-boiled egg whites through a fine strainer; mix with Mixture A. Place in oblong mold (size: 2 cup capacity); press. **(1)**
2. Mash yolks with back of fork; mix with Mixture B. Put through sieve. Put 3 tablespoons of yolk aside, being careful not to destroy crumbly texture. Place remaining yolk on top of white in mold; press. **(2)**
3. Top (2) with 3 tablespoons yolk sprinkled through strainer held above mold; tap strainer with side of wooden spoon or spatula. **(3)**
4. Lay large dish towel in hot steam cooker to facilitate removal of mold when done. Place mold on towel; cover top of container with cloth; put lid on.
5. Steam over medium heat 15 minutes. **(4)**
6. Remove mold from steam cooker; cool. Take out of mold; cut into 5 fan-shaped pieces. Insert toothpicks into each as fan handles. Garnish with *kinomé* or watercress.

Snow White Jelly (*Awayuki kan*)

いちご入り泡雪かん

Ingredients:
1 stick agar-agar
2½ cups water
1½–2 cups sugar
2 egg whites
6–8 strawberries
1 tablespoon lemon juice
small amount of grated lemon rind

Substitute for Agar-agar: 2 tablespoons unflavored gelatin
1 cup water
1½ cups sugar

In double boiler, soften gelatin in 1 cup of water for a few minutes, add sugar and cook until completely dissolved. Then follow above recipe from No. 5.

The gelatin is ready when a drop forms a small ball in cold water.

Method:

1. Tear agar-agar into pieces. Wash in water; squeeze out water. Soak in 2½ cups water 30 minutes. **(1)**
2. Cook over medium heat, stir gently with wooden spoon till agar-agar is dissolved. Strain through damp cheesecloth. **(2)**
3. Return to pan. Add sugar; cook over low heat.
4. Simmer, skimming off scum until reduced to half original quantity. Stand chopstick in pan to test quantity.
5. Meanwhile, wash and stem strawberries; wipe. Wet mold (size: 5 cup capacity) or individual cups.
6. Beat whites in dry bowl until stiff. Gradually beat in agar-agar mixture, grated lemon rind and juice. Keep on beating until slightly thickened. **(3–4)**
7. Pour into mold. Insert strawberries. Refrigerate till set. **(5–6)**
8. Take out of mold. Cut into squares. Place on plate arranged with green leaves. Serve with custard sauce, if desired.

Typical Japanese Menu

Continued on pages 67-71

Clear Soup with Flower-Shaped Prawn, White Meat Fish Roasted in Foil, Boiled Chicken Meatballs with Turnips, Crab and Cucumber Salad with *Kimizu* Dressing, Rice with Green Peas

Yakitori
Party

*Continued on
pages 72-75*

Egg Soup,
Japanese Chicken
Kebab,
Japanese Style
Salad,
Rice Balls

Teppan-yaki
Menu

Continued on pages 76-79

Fried Lotus Root, Grilled Meat and Vegetables, String Beans with *Goma* Sauce, Okra *Misoshiru*

Sakana for *Sake*

Continued on pages 80-83

**Cucumber with
Japanese Bean
Paste,
Grilled Mushrooms,
Salmon Roe with
Grated *Daikon*,
Vinegared Fish**

58

Cake and Japanese Tea

Continued on pages 84-85

**Steamed Ginger Cake,
Japanese Tea**

Cutting and Slicing—
The Japanese Way

See page 10

64

Typical Japanese Menu

Continued from page 52

Clear Soup with Flower-Shaped Prawn
(*Hana-ebi no Sumashi-jiru*)
花えびのすまし汁

White Meat Fish Roasted in Foil
(*Shiromi no Sakana no Gingami Tsutsumi-yaki*)
白身の魚の銀紙焼き

Boiled Chicken Meatballs with Turnips
(*Tori-dango to Kokabu no Nimono*)
鶏だんごと小かぶの煮物

Crab and Cucumber Salad with *Kimi-zu* Dressing
(*Kani to Kyuri no Kimizu-ae*)
かにときゅうりの黄身酢あえ

Rice with Green Peas
(*Aomame Gohan*)
青豆ごはん

Soup Stock (*Dashi*) *

The best soup stock used for clear soups and certain recipes is "*Ichiban* (first) *Dashi*." In this book it is called "*Dashi*." The second soup stock used for ordinary cooking is called "*Niban* (second) *Dashi*."

DASHI (Bonito Soup)

Ingredients for 4 cups *dashi*;
1–2 cups shaved dried bonito
1 piece *dashi-kombu* (kelp seaweed)
    (4″–8″ long)
5 cups water

First wipe sand off dried kelp, leaving the white powder on kelp (it is tasty). Make several crosswise cuts. These cuts will help to draw out the flavor.

1. Put kelp in pan with 5 cups water. Let stand for 1 hour. Cook over medium heat. Remove kelp just before boiling point to avoid kelp odor.
2. When it comes to a boil, lower heat, add bonito shavings.
3. Boil 30 seconds to 1 minute, skimming off scum. Turn off heat.
4. Set aside. As soon as shavings have settled to bottom, strain through cheesecloth.

NIBAN DASHI (Second Soup Stock)

Use the kelp and bonito shavings already used once in making *dashi*.

In pan, put kelp, shavings and 2–4 cups water (according to amount needed). Bring to a boil. Remove kelp just before it comes to boiling point. Keep on boiling 3–4 minutes. Strain through cheesecloth.

KOMBU DASHI (Kelp Stock)

In 4 cups water, soak 6″ length kelp prepared as for *dashi* for 3 hours. Bring to a boil. Remove kelp. Skim off scum.

NIBOSHI DASHI (Dried Fish Soup)

This soup stock is used for *Miso* Soup (Japanese Bean Paste Soup).

Ingredients for 4 cups *Niboshi Dashi*:
15 *niboshi* (dried small fish)
1 piece *dashi-kombu* (kelp seaweed)
  (4″ long)
1 tablespoon *sake*
1 piece sliced fresh ginger (or green onion)
4½ cups water

Remove heads and entrails from *niboshi*. If *niboshi* are large, remove center bones also. Put all ingredients in pan. Let stand at least for 30 minutes. Bring to a boil; remove kelp just before boiling point. Lower heat; cook for 15–20 minutes, skimming off scum. Strain through cheesecloth.

Clear Soup with Flower-Shaped Prawn
(*Hana-ebi no Sumashi-jiru*)

花えびのすまし汁

Ingredients:

8 prawns
2 tablespoons *katakuriko* or cornstarch
2 cups *niban-dashi* (second soup stock)
4 fresh *shiitake* caps, crisscrossed on top with knife
8 stalks fresh asparagus
a little salt, *mirin and* MSG to taste
4 cups *dashi* (bonito soup)
1 teaspoon soy sauce
4 *kinomé* or *yuzu* rind (lime or lemon can be substituted for *yuzu*)

Method:

1. Shell prawns, leaving tail. With sharp knife, make a shallow cut along outside curve of prawn; open; then remove black vein. Make a ½″ slit in center, insert tail through hole, pull out from opposite side so it will look like a flower.
2. Sprinkle prawns with *katakuriko* or cornstarch. Cook lightly in salted boiling *niban dashi*. Remove prawns.
3. Cook *shiitake* lightly in *niban-dashi*.
4. Cut only asparagus tips into 2″ piece lengthwise. Cook lightly in salted boiling water. Drain in colander; sprinkle with salt, *mirin* and MSG.
5. Place prawns, *shiitake* and asparagus in individual serving soup bowls. Bring *dashi*, salt, soy sauce to a boil and pour into soup bowls. Garnish with *kinomé* or a small piece of *yuzu* rind.

67

White Meat Fish Roasted in Foil

白身の魚の銀紙焼き

(*Shiromi no Sakana no Gingami Tsutsumi-yaki*)

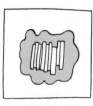

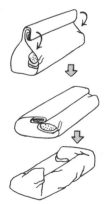

Ingredients:

1 onion, sliced crosswise

4 slices white meat fish (or ½ lb. chicken fillet), each slice cut into 3 pieces

2 green peppers, quartered and seeded

4 fresh *shiitake* caps, crisscrossed on top with knife

4 teaspoon *sake*

1 teaspoon salt

1 teaspoon fresh ginger juice

4 slices lemon

4 sheets (size: 14″×10″) aluminum foil

4 sheets (size: 4″×3½″) aluminum foil

salad oil for greasing foil

Method:

1. Place smaller foil in middle of larger foil sheet. Grease center with salad oil. On top of foil, place in this order; onion slices, fish, green peppers and *shiitake*.

2. Sprinkle each portion of fish with 1 teaspoon *sake*, ¼ teaspoon salt and ginger juice. Top with a slice of lemon. Wrap tightly.

3. Preheat a frying pan over medium heat. Place wrapped fish in pan, cover. Roast about 12–13 minutes (or bake in oven, heated to 425°F.)

4. Serve hot with lemon juice or soy sauce.

Boiled Chicken Meatballs with Turnips 鶏だんごと小かぶの煮物
(*Tori-dango to Kokabu no Nimono*)

Ingredients:

1 piece *dashi kombu* (8″ long)

3½ cups water

8 turnips

4 dried *shiitake*, stemmed, softened in water

9 oz. ground chicken

Mixture A:

   1 tablespoon *sake*

   ½ teaspoon salt

   1 teaspoon sugar

   1 tablespoon cornstarch

1 egg

3–4 *kikurage* (cloud-ear mushrooms), if desired, soaked in water, drained and cut into thin strips

2 oz. carrots, cut into thin strips

1 teaspoon minced fresh ginger

Mixture B:

   2 tablespoons *sake*

   ½ teaspoon salt

   2 tablespoons sugar

   3 tablespoons soy sauce

2 oz. snow peas, cooked in salted boiling water, drained and sprinkled with salt, *mirin* and MSG.

a little *yuzu* rind or thin strips of ginger

Method:

1. Prepare *kombu dashi* with 3½ cups water and *dashi kombu* as on page 65.
2. Cut off turnip greens, leaving ½″ of stems. Wash well. Peel and cut into halves lengthwise; then make incision at root end to about ½″ of top of turnips.
3. Make crisscross cuts on top of *shiitake*.
4. Grind chicken meat in *suribachi* (a mortar) or electric blender; mix in Mixture A and slightly beaten egg. Blend in *kikurage*, carrots and ginger.
5. Bring *kombu dashi* to a boil. Remove *kombu* just before boiling point. Skim off scum. Add Mixture B. Drop meat mixture into boiling *kombu dashi*. Use 2 teaspoons to shape meat mixture into balls (about 1¼″ in diameter). (Dip spoons into water before using to prevent meat from sticking.)
6. Add turnips and *shiitake*. To keep steam down, place a smaller lid on top of meatballs before covering pan with its own cover. Reduce heat, cook until turnips become tender.
7. Serve on plate. Garnish with snow peas and *yuzu* rind or ginger strips.

69

Crab and Cucumber Salad with *Kimizu* Dressing

(*Kani to Kyuri no Kimizu-ae*)

かにときゅうりの黄身酢あえ

Ingredients:

1 can (7 oz.) crab meat
a little vinegar
2 small cucumbers
a little salt
Kimi-zu Dressing:
   2 egg yolks
   ⅔ teaspoon salt
   1½ tablespoons sugar
   ½ teaspoon cornstarch
   4 tablespoons *dashi* (bonito soup)
   2 tablespoons vinegar
   seasoning

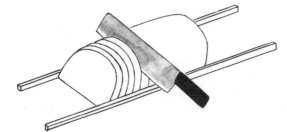

Method:

1. Remove cartilage from crab meat; flake; sprinkle with vinegar.
2. Rub salt into cucumbers by rolling on cutting board. Slice as pictured. Then cut crosswise into ½″ pieces. Sprinkle with salt. Let stand a few minutes. Wash and squeeze out.
3. Make *Kimi-zu* as on page 90.
4. Serve crab meat and cucumbers in individual serving bowls. Pour *Kimi-zu* Dressing over all.

Rice with Green Peas (*Aomame Gohan*)

青豆ごはん

Ingredients:
2 cups rice
2 cups *kombu dashi* (kelp soup)
2 teaspoons salt
1 tablespoon *sake*
1 cup green peas

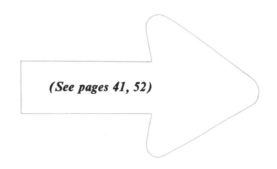

(See pages 41, 52)

Method:
1. Wash rice. Put it in heavy pot with *kombu dashi*, salt, *sake*. Let stand for 1 hour.
2. Add peas to rice, just before cooking. Cook as on page 89. Let rice stand in pot with lid on for 15 minutes after cooked.
3. Fluff rice up with wooden spatula or fork before serving.

Chestnut Rice (*Kuri Gohan*)

くりごはん

Ingredients:
3 cups rice
3¼ cups water
2 tablespoons *sake*
1 tablespoon salt
1 piece *dashi kombu* (6″ long); make several cuts
1 ½ cups chestnuts
1 tablespoon toasted black sesame seeds

Method:
1. Wash rice, drain. Put rice, water, *sake*, salt, *dashi kombu* in heavy pan; let stand 1 hour.
2. Shell and skin chestnuts. Soak in water 30 minutes.
3. Just before cooking, drain chestnuts, add to rice. Cover and cook over high heat until it comes to a boil. Remove *kombu*. Cover again. After 30 seconds, lower heat and simmer 12–13 minutes. Let stand 13 minutes. Fluff up with wooden spatula or fork. Sprinkle with toasted black sesame seeds.

The best soup stock used for clear soups and certain recipes is "*Ichiban* (first) *Dashi*." In this book it is called "*Dashi*." The second soup stock used for ordinary cooking is called "*Niban* (second) *Dashi*."

Yakitori Party

Coutinued from page 54

Egg Soup
(*Otoshi Tamago no Sumashi*)
落とし卵のすまし
Japanese Chicken Kebab
(*Yakitori*)
焼とり
Japanese Style Salad
(*Wafu* Salad)
和風サラダ
Rice Balls
(*Onigiri*)
おにぎり

Egg Soup (*Otoshi Tamago no Sumashi*)　　　落とし卵のすまし

6 cups *dashi* (bonito soup)
2 teaspoons salt
1–1½ teaspoons soy sauce
yuzu rind, shredded (see page 10)

Method:
1. Leaving about 1½″ of stem, cut off spinach roots. Wash well. Plunge in boiling water with 1 teaspoon sugar (do not overcook). Soak in cold water.
2. In pan, put 5 cups water, 1 teaspoon salt, 3 tablespoons vinegar. Bring to a boil. Lower heat; add one egg. Boil 4–5 minutes. Remove and put into lukewarm water. Repeat. Drain.
3. Bring *dashi* and salt to a boil, add soy sauce. Place each egg in individual bowls with spinach. Fill hot soup, garnish with *yuzu* rind.

Ingredients:
8 stalks spinach
1 teaspoon sugar
6 eggs
5 cups water
1 teaspoon salt
3 tablespoons vinegar

Japanese Chicken Kebab (*Yakitori*)

焼とり

Ingredients:

3 green onions, cut into 1″ strips lengthwise
   (or 16 small onions, cooked in salted boiling
   water)
8 green peppers, quartered and seeded
⅔ lb. chicken livers
1 clove garlic
1⅓ lb. boned chicken breast
Barbecue Sauce:
   ½ cup soy sauce
   ½ cup *mirin*
   1–2 tablespoons sugar
sansho powder or pepper
bamboo skewers or sticks

Method:

1. Pierce skewer through sides of green onions. Skewer green peppers in the same way.
2. Cut livers into 4–6 pieces. Soak in water to remove odor.
3. Crush garlic, add to 5 cups boiling water; add livers (do not overcook), drain in colander. Skewer livers.
4. Remove skin of chicken. Cut into bite-size pieces.
5. Cook skin in boiling water, cut into 1¼″ × ¾″ pieces, put on skewers.
6. Arrange skewers on platter.
7. Simmer Barbecue Sauce until reduced to half of original quantity.
8. Place gridiron over high heat, arrange two bricks on both sides. Barbecue, brushing with sauce, until cooked as desired. Sprinkle with *sansho* powder or pepper. Let guests help themselves.

Japanese Style Salad
(*Wafu* Salad)

和風サラダ

Ingredients:

1 can (7 oz.) crab meat, cartilage removed and flaked

1 carrot (2″ long); cut into very thin strips and soak in water

1 cucumber; rub in salt by rolling on cutting board and shred

2 green onions or 1 poireau; shred lengthwise, wrap in cheesecloth and wash

10 radishes; cut into thin crosswise slices and shred

1 head of lettuce

Dressing:

   3 tablespoons white sesame seeds

   Mayonnaise and Vinegar Mixture:

      ¼ teaspoon grated garlic

      2 tablespoons mayonnaise

      a dash of cayenne pepper

      1 tablespoon soy sauce

      5 tablespoons vinegar

      4 tablespoons *dashi* (bonito soup)

      ¼ teaspoon salt

      a dash of MSG (optional)

Method:

1. Drain soaked vegetables, dry. Combine prepared crab meat and vegetables. Place in lettuce-lined bowl. Cover with cellophane. Refrigerate till serving.

2. Dressing: Toast sesame seeds over low heat and grind. Stir in Mayonnaise and Vinegar Mixture.

3. Serve salad with Dressing.

Rice Balls (*Onigiri*)

おにぎり

Ingredients:
3 cups rice
3¼ cups water
4 sheets dried *nori* (seaweed)
4–5 *umeboshi* (pickled plums)
2 teaspoons black sesame seeds
salt
aonori (crushed green seaweed)

Method:
1. Wash rice 1 hour before cooking.
2. Cook and fluff up rice as on page 86.
3. Toast *nori* by holding it over low heat. Cut 2 sheets of *nori* into 9 strips (about ¾″ wide). Cut the other 2 sheets into 8 strips (about 1″ wide).
4. Take out pit from *umeboshi* and cut into small pieces.
5. Toast sesame seeds in pan over low heat.
6. Divide rice into two parts for 2 kinds of rice balls.
7. Triangular rice balls: Wet hands, and sprinkle with salt. Mold handful of rice into triangular shape, sprinkle with sesame seeds. Press a piece of *umeboshi* into center. Put a ¾″ band of *nori* around outer edge of triangle.
8. Oblong rice balls: Make remaining half of rice into round oblong shapes. Put a 1″ band of *nori* around middle. You may sprinkle one end with sesame seeds and the other end with *aonori*, if desired.

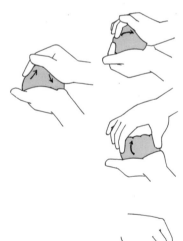

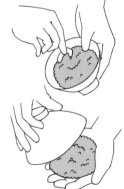

Teppan-yaki Menu

Continued from page 56

Fried Lotus Root
(*Age Renkon*)
揚げ蓮根

Grilled Meat and Vegetables
(*Teppan-yaki*)
鉄板焼き

String Beans with *Goma* Sauce
(*Ingen no Goma-ae*)
いんげんのごまあえ

Okra *Miso* Soup
(*Okura no Misoshiru*)
オクラのみそ汁

Fried Lotus Root

(*Age Renkon*)

揚げ蓮根

Ingredients:
2 oz. lotus roots; pare and cut into paper-thin
   crosswise slices
1 teaspoon salt
12 ginkgo nuts; shell and skin (4″ × ½″)
8 pieces of *dashi-kombu*
salad oil for deep-frying
salt and pepper

Method:
1. Soak lotus root slices in water with 1 teaspoon salt for 1 hour. Drain. Wipe and dry completely. Heat oil to about 330°F. (low heat). Deep-fry. When crispy, remove from oil (if not crisp enough, fry again in very hot oil). Sprinkle with salt and pepper.
2. Skewer three ginkgo nuts on toothpick. Tie *kombu* strips as pictured. Fry nuts and *kombu*. Sprinkle with salt and pepper.

How to Shell and Skin Ginkgo Nuts:
Shell gingko nuts with nut cracker or crack with back of knife. In small sauce pan, bring to a boil just enough salt water to cover gingko nuts. Add nuts, scrape off skin by rubbing in pan with back of slotted spoon or ladle.

76

Grilled Meat and Vegetables

(*Teppan-yaki*)

鉄板焼き

Ingredients:
2 onions, sliced ½" thick
1 eggplant, cut into ½" crosswise slices
1 lb. beef tenderloin, cut into ⅕" slices
4–8 prawns, shelled (with tails) and deveined
2 green peppers, quartered and seeded
8 fresh *shiitake* caps
3–4 cabbage leaves, shredded
salad oil

Seasonings:
Goma-zu Sauce:
   3 tablespoons white or black sesame seeds
   Soy Sauce Mixture:
      6 tablespoons soy sauce
      2 tablespoons *mirin*
      2 tablespoons lemon juice
      2 tablespoons *dashi*
Ponzu Sauce:
   juice of 1 lemon
   soy sauce
6 tablespoons *Momiji-Oroshi*, (see page 82)

Preparations:
1. Push toothpick through center of each onion slice to keep rings together.
2. Soak eggplant slices in cold water about 20 minutes. Drain; then dry well.
3. Arrange meat, prawns and vegetables artistically on large platter.
4. To make *Goma-zu* Sauce: Toast sesame seeds in hot unoiled pan over low heat. Shake pan constantly. Be careful not to overbrown seeds. Grind until smooth. Blend in Soy Sauce Mixture.
5. To make Ponzu Sauce: Dilute lemon juice with equal quantity of soy sauce.

Table Cooking:
Preheat large skillet over high heat on table. Grease with salad oil. Grill portions of meat, prawns and vegetables. Serve and eat while cooking. Let guests choose their favorite dip.

77

String Beans with *Goma* Sauce

(Ingen no Goma-ae)

いんげんのごまあえ

Ingredients:
½ lb. string beans, sliced diagonally ⅕″ thick
2 teaspoons salt
Mixture A:
   ¼ teaspoon salt
   1 teaspoon *mirin*
   ¼ teaspoon MSG (optional)
Goma Sauce:
   4 tablespoons white sesame seeds
Mixture B:
   1 tablespoon sugar
   1 tablespoon soy sauce
   1–2 tablespoons *dashi* (bonito soup)

Method:
1. Cook string beans in 5 cups boiling water
   with 2 teaspoons salt. Drain immediately.
   Sprinkle with Mixture A. Cool.
2. To make *Goma* Sauce: Toast sesame seeds
   over low heat; grind; blend in Mixture B.
3. Mix string beans with *Goma* Sauce.

Okra *Miso* Soup
(*Okura no Misoshiru*)

オクラのみそ汁

Ingredients:
4–8 pods of okra
4 cups *dashi* (bonito soup)
3–4 tablespoons *miso*
½ green onion, shredded
a little salt

Method:
1. Rub salt into okra. Cut into ¼″ crosswise slices.
2. Bring *dashi* to a boil and add okra. Dissolve *miso* in *dashi* and add to soup. Bring to a boil. Turn off heat. Sprinkle with green onion. Serve immediately.

Sakana for *Sake*

Continued from page 58

Cucumber with Japanese Bean Paste
(*Morokyu*)
もろきゅう
Grilled Mushrooms
(*Nama-jiitake no Tsuke-yaki*)
生じいたけのつけ焼き
Salmon Roe with Grated *Daikon*
(*Ikura to daikon no Oroshi-ae*)
イクラのおろしあえ
Vinegared Fish
(*Kisu no Sujime*)
きすの酢じめ

Cucumber with Japanese Bean Paste
(*Morokyu*)

もろきゅう

Ingredients:
8–12 small cucumbers (or 2 ordinary size cucumbers)
4 tablespoons *moromi-miso* or *miso*

Method:
Rub salt into cucumbers, rolling them on cutting board. Place in flat colander. Pour boiling water over. Soak in cold water immediately. Cut into thin slices crosswise. Serve with *miso*. Celery stalks may be substituted for cucumbers.

Grilled Mushrooms

(*Nama-jiitake no Tsuke-yaki*)

生じいたけのつけ焼き

Ingredients:
12 radishes or 4 small turnips
Vinegar Sauce:
   3 tablespoons vinegar
   ⅓ teaspoon salt
   1½ tablespoons sugar
3 fresh *shiitake*
Basting Sauce:
   1 tablespoon soy sauce
   1 tablespoon *mirin*
a dash of cayenne pepper

Method:
1. Prepare radishes as in "*Kikka-kabu*" (see page 91). Soak in Vinegar Sauce for 1 hour.
2. Cut off stems of *shiitake*. Wash and drain. Grill lightly top side up on greased gridiron; turn over. Baste with soy sauce and Basting Sauce. Turn over again; grill slowly, while basting. Sprinkle with cayenne pepper.
3. Serve *shiitake* with radishes garnished with chrysanthemum leaves, if desired.

Salmon Roe with Grated *Daikon*
(*Ikura to Daikon no Oroshi-aé*)

イクラのおろしあえ

Ingredients:
½ cup grated *daikon*
Vinegar Mixture:
   3 tablespoons vinegar
   1½ tablespoons sugar
   ½ teaspoon salt
2 tablespoons salmon roe
½ teaspoon minced parsley

Method:
1. If grated *daikon* tastes too strong, wrap in cheesecloth, wash and squeeze out lightly. Combine with Vinegar Mixture.
2. Combine salmon roe with grated *daikon*. Serve in individual serving bowls. Sprinkle with parsley.

Variation:
Serve salmon roe and grated *daikon* mixture on lemon slices. Sprinkle with lemon juice. Top with minced parsley or scoop out lemon and fill shells with salmon roe and grated *daikon* mixture.

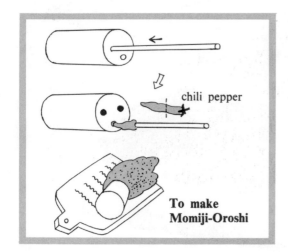

chili pepper

**To make
Momiji-Oroshi**

Vinegared Fish
(*Kisu no Sujime*)

きすの酢じめ

Ingredients:

4 *kisu* (sillaginoids) or smelt
1 teaspoon salt
a little vinegar
Vinegar Mixture:
   3 tablespoons vinegar
   1 tablespoon *mirin*
   ½ teaspoon salt
   1 tablespoon sugar
1 cucumber
1 teaspoon salt
½ piece fresh ginger, grated

Method:

1. Cut *kisu* into 3 fillets as on page 88. Wash and drain in flat colander. Sprinkle with 1 teaspoon salt. Let stand for 20 minutes. Then, soak in enough vinegar to cover for 10 minutes. Remove skin. Cut fish into ¼″ wide diagonal slices.
2. Bring Vinegar Mixture to a boil. Cool.
3. Rub salt into cucumber by rolling on cutting board. Wash. Cut into halves lengthwise. Spoon out seeds. Cut into thin slices. Sprinkle with 1 teaspoon salt. Let stand a few minutes. Rinse under cold water. Squeeze out water. Combine with fish. Pour Vinegar Mixture over everything.

If you have a yellow chrysanthemum on hand, pluck off petals and wash. Bring 3 cups water to a boil, add 2 tablespoons vinegar and petals. Remove from heat immediately. Soak in cold water, drain and squeeze out. Add petals to vinegar mixture. Garnish *kisu* and cucumbers artistically with petals and chrysanthemum leaves, if desired.

Cake and Japanese Tea

Continued from page 60

Steamed Ginger Cake
(*Kuroiso*)
黒磯
Japanese Tea
(*Nihon Cha*)
日本茶

Steamed Ginger Cake

(*Kuroiso*)

黒磯

Ingredients:

1 cup flour
1½ teaspoons baking powder
1 medium egg
3 tablespoons chopped walnuts
⅔ cup chunky brown sugar or, if preferred
   dark molasses
4 tablespoons warm water
1 teaspoon fresh ginger juice or 1 teaspoon
   ginger powder
½ teaspoon white sesame seeds
1 tablespoon sugar
salad oil

Method:

1. Line 7″×3″ baking tin with paper, then grease with salad oil.
2. Place steam cooker with water over high heat. (A basket set into a deep pan will also act as a steamer).
3. Sift flour and baking powder.
4. Dissolve chunky brown sugar in warm water. (If ordinary brown sugar is used, this step is unnecessary.) Cool.
5. Beat egg, mix in 1 tablespoon sugar.
6. Add ginger juice and egg to brown sugar. Blend in sifted flour (3). Mix in walnuts.
7. Pour batter in tin. Place in hot steam cooker. Put a towel between lid and cooker, taking care that it does not hang down near heat. Steam over high heat about 30–35 minutes or until skewer inserted in center comes out clean.
8. Toast sesame seeds in pan over low heat. Chop and sprinkle over cake.
9. Remove from tin, cool on rack. Slice to serve.

The same dough may be baked in oven instead of steamer. Heat oven to 370°F. Set tin in shallow baking pan; place on oven rack. Fill pan with hot water. Bake for about 20–25 minutes in preheated oven.

How to Serve Good Japanese Tea

日本茶

Japanese tea may be divided into 4 general groups—*Matcha*, *Gyokuro*, *Sencha*, and *Bancha*, which are served on different occasions and brewed in different ways.

Matcha: This is a powdered green tea made from superior grade tea leaves. It is used in "A Tea Ceremony."

Gyokuro and Sencha: These are also made from high quality tea leaves and are therefore served to guests.

Bancha: This is the most popular tea leaf for home use.

To Serve *Gyokuro*:

5 servings
2 tablespoons *gyokuro* tea
½–¾ cup boiling water
some hot water

Gyokuro has a strong aroma. The taste seems a little bitter at first but it mellows as it remains on the tongue. This tea is not the type to drink like water but is drunk a little at a time to enjoy the flavor. Use a dainty teapot with matching cups when serving. In Japan there are special small sets for *gyokuro*.

Put measured boiling water in separate container. Set aside. Meanwhile warm teapot by filling with water. Have your cups in a line on a tray at table, pour hot water from teapot, filling each cup.

Empty teapot. Measure tea leaves into teapot, pour in warm water from separate container (cooled to 140°F.–160°F.) Let stand for 1½ minutes.

Empty warmed tea cups. Swish tea in teapot. Pouring tea through strainer, half fill cups in succession. Fill the last cup to ⅔ and reverse the order till the last drop has been emptied from teapot.

Wipe the bottom of cups and serve on saucers. (Japanese saucers are usually lacquer ware).

When you want to use the same tea leaves for a second infusion use a little warmer water than the first time and let it stand only a minute; swish.

To Serve *Sencha*:

5 servings
2 tablespoons *sencha* tea
1–1¼ cups boiling water

Use a little larger teapot and tea cups than for *gyokuro*. *Sencha* is brewed almost the same as *gyokuro*, but the temperature of the water should be a little higher (170°F.–175°F.), and the time of infusion a little shorter (40 seconds to 1 minute).

To Serve *Bancha*:

5 servings
3 tablespoons *bancha* tea
2½–3 cups boiling water

There are many kinds of *bancha*. To extract the flavor from tea leaves, roast the leaves in pan over low heat before serving. Use a large teapot and tea cups. Put the leaves in teapot. Add boiling water. Pour into tea cups after 10 seconds of infusion. Do not pour in more boiling water than needed. If tea is drained to the last drop, you may use leaves a second time, but the flavor is slightly changed.

(Continued from page 43) ✳

Vinegared Rice Rolled in *Nori*
(Nori-maki)

Thick *Norimaki*:
1. Place a bamboo screen (size: $10'' \times 9\frac{1}{2}''$) or dry cloth. Dry *nori* over low heat. Put a sheet of *nori* (shiny side down) on screen flush with the edge of screen facing you. Wet your hands in equal quantities of water and vinegar to handle rice easier. Spread $1\frac{1}{2}$ cups vinegared rice evenly on *nori*, leaving $\frac{1}{2}''$ space at far edge. On top of rice, place in the following order; *kampyo* strips, egg sticks, fish flakes, *mitsuba*, carrot and *shiitake*. Leave $\frac{1}{4}$ of rice uncovered on opposite side, as pictured.   **(1–2)**
2. Roll rice as in picture (page 43).
3. Wrap roller tightly around *norimaki* to shape.   **(3–5)**
4. Stand *norimaki* (still in rolled screen) on cutting board, tap it to compress it. Insert fingers from top and push end of *norimaki* lightly to flatten and shape. Do this on both ends.
5. Unroll by lifting rolled screen higher and higher with one hand as you guide *norimaki* roll out with the other hand. Finish with open end of *norimaki* at bottom. Make 4 thick rolls.

Thin *Norimaki*:
1. Cut 1 sheet of *nori* into halves crosswise.
2. Place half sheet of *nori* lengthwise on roller as previously explained for thick *norimaki*. Spread $\frac{1}{2}$ cup vinegared rice evenly on *nori*. Place 3 or 4 *kampyo* strips in center of rice.
3. First fold in half and then roll as for thick *norimaki*.

To Cut:
Dip cheesecloth in vinegared water; wring out. Wipe knife with cloth, then cut *norimaki* in cross sections. Cut straight down, then pull the knife towards you. Do not cut back and forth.   **(6)**

To Serve:
Arrange slices artistically on large platter or individual serving dishes, with cut sides up. Garnish with sweet vinegared ginger and green leaves.

Thin Egg Omelet

(Usuyaki Tamago)

薄焼き卵

Ingredients:
2 eggs
⅓ teaspoon salt
2 teaspoons sugar
a dash of MSG

Method:

1. Beat eggs. Stir in salt, sugar and MSG. Pour mixture through fine strainer.
2. Heat skillet over medium heat. Grease skillet thoroughly with oiled paper towel.
3. Pour in ⅓–¼ of egg mixture, tilt skillet to spread mixture evenly.
4. When surface of egg mixture begins to dry, use chopsticks to loosen edges.
5. Remove skillet from heat, insert chopstick about ⅓ under egg sheet on far edge. Lift up sheet and turn over. Place skillet on heat again, remove egg sheet as soon as it dries. Place on cutting board. Do not lay one on top another while hot, otherwise they will stick together. Cut into halves, then into strips.

To Cut Fish into Three Sections

1. Place head of fish toward your left, scale from tail side upward to head.
2. Insert point of knife under gill cover, pull out gills.
3. Make a slit near pectoral fin, remove entrails.
4. Bind 4 or 5 toothpicks together with rubber band and use this to scrape around backbone to clean.
5. Wash in salt water.
6. Cut into 3 sections as pictured. Place on flat colander.

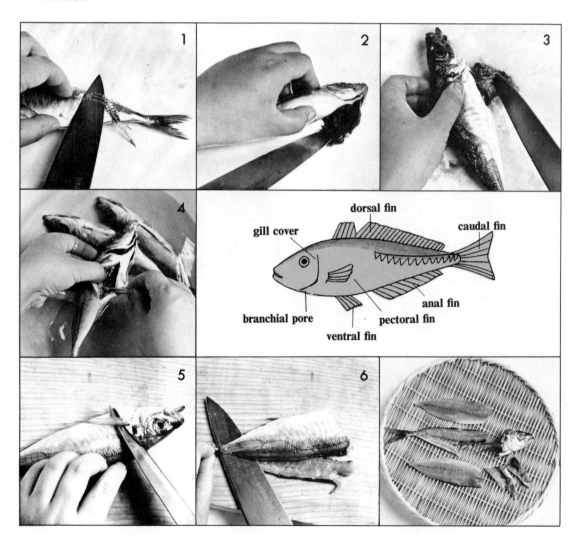

To Cook Rice

Type and Size of Pot:
A deep, heavy pot with a heavy lid is the best for cooking rice, because rice water has a tendency to boil over. The size of pot is also very important. As rice expands about 2½ times during cooking, choose a pot that has 4 times the depth of the amount of raw rice. If the pot is too small and the lid not heavy enough, the rice will boil over and also will not expand sufficiently.

To Wash Rice:
Rice absorbs 10% water in the first 5 minutes, 80% in 1 hour, and 100% in 3 hours. So it is best to wash rice 3 hours ahead of cooking, but when you do not have enough time, try to wash it at least an hour ahead of cooking. Place rice in a bowl or pan. Fill a large bowl with water and pour it over rice. Wash rice, pour out water immediately. (Do not wash under running water, or the odor of rice-bran will remain.) Wash rice well in 3 or 4 changes of cold water until water becomes clear. Drain into colander.

Amount of Water to Add:
First put rice in cooking pot. The amount of water to be added then varies with the kind of rice.

For polished rice: Add 15–20% more water than rice.

For new rice (the first crop of rice for the year): add the same amount of 15–20% more water than rice.

For old rice (long-stored rice): Add 20–30% more water than rice.

When the pot to be used for cooking rice is thin or the amount of rice is small, add a little more water than usual. Soak from 1–3 hours.

To Cook:
1. First cook covered over high heat. (Do not remove lid at any time during cooking.) Adjust heat to bring rice to boiling point in 10–15 minutes. (When the amount of rice is small, cook over lower heat than usual to allow more cooking time.)
2. When rice starts to boil, reduce heat just enough to keep it at a gentle boil.
3. Simmer for 10–13 minutes, or until all water is absorbed. Turn heat to high for 30 seconds, then turn off.
4. Let rice stand in pot with lid on for 12–15 minutes. (If you see small holes on surface of rice, your rice is cooked well.)
5. It is best to turn cooked rice into a wooden container. If it is to be left in pot, fluff it up with a wooden spatula or fork, and put a dishcloth between lid and pot to absorb moisture.

Vinegared Rice for "_SUSHI_"
3 cups rice
3¼ cups water
1 piece _dashi kombu_ (4″ long), cut with a few slits
Vinegar Mixture:
    4½ tablespoons vinegar
    2–3 teaspoons sugar
    2 teaspoons salt
    a dash of MSG

1. Especially when preparing vinegared rice, rice should be washed well, 1 hour ahead cooking time.
2. Put rice in pot, add water (a little more than the amount of rice) and _dashi-kombu_. Cook covered over high heat, bring to a boil. Remove _kombu_ and cover again. After 30 seconds lower heat and simmer 12–13 minutes.
3. Turn off heat. Let rice stand for not more than 12 minutes. Turn into a wooden bowl. Pour Vinegar Mixture over rice and sprinkle with MSG. While fluffing rice up with wooden spatula, fan to cool until lukewarm. (This helps rice absorb vinegar mixture quickly.) For easy handling, use vinegared rice before it becomes cold. Cover bowl with damp cloth to keep warm.

Salad Dressing, Sauces and Dips

SAMBAI-ZU

{
3 tablespoons vinegar
1 teaspoon soy sauce
1 tablespoon sugar
½ teaspoon salt

Mix all ingredients together. This is the most popular Japanese salad dressing.

NIHAI-ZU

{
3 tablespoons vinegar
2 tablespoons soy sauce
½ teaspoon salt

Mix all ingredients together. This salad dressing is mostly used for fish and shellfish.

KIMI-ZU

{
2 egg yolks
⅔ teaspoon salt
1½ tablespoons sugar
½ teaspoon cornstarch
4 tablespoons *dashi*
2 tablespoons vinegar

In double boiler, beat yolk slightly; mix in salt, sugar, cornstarch. Gradually stir in *dashi* and vinegar. Continue cooking, stirring constantly until thickened. This is a kind of Japanese mayonnaise.

GOMA-ZU (Sesame Seed Dressing)

{
4 tablespoons black sesame seeds
1 tablespoon sugar
1½–2 tablespoons soy sauce
1 tablespoon *sake*
2 tablespoons vinegar

Toast sesame seeds in unoiled pan over low heat; grind until smooth. Blend in all ingredients. Stir in 1 tablespoon *dashi* or liquid from cooked vegetable, if desired.

TARE

Boil equal quantities of soy sauce and *mirin*. Simmer until reduced by ⅔ of original quantity. Pour in glass jar when cool. Store covered in refrigerator. It is delicious to use for basting broiled or grilled chicken, meat, fish, shrimp, etc.

PONZU SAUCE

Pare off ½″ wide peel from around *daidai* (orange) center. Cut crosswise at pared area (this is to avoid bitterness of peel). Squeeze out juice; dilute with equal quantity of soy sauce. This is a popular dip served with *Mizutaki* recipe.

TENTSUYU SAUCE

{
1 cup *dashi*
¼–⅓ cup soy sauce
¼–⅓ cup *mirin*

Bring ingredients to boiling point. The quantity of soy sauce and *mirin* varies with personal taste. Serve with *Tempura*.

Vinegared Fresh Ginger
SUDORI-SHOGA

5–6 stalks young fresh ginger
Vinegar Mixture:
   ½ cup vinegar
   4 tablespoons sugar
   1 teaspoon salt
   ¼ cup water

Bring Vinegar Mixture to a boil. Cool. Pour mixture into a glass. Cut leaves off fresh ginger, leaving about 9″ of stem. Clean roots. Dip only the roots into boiling salted water. Remove immediately. Shake off water. Dip in Vinegar Mixture while hot.

Sweet Vinegared Ginger
AMAZUKE-SHOGA

Pare ginger. Soak in water. Cut thinly. Cook lightly in boiling water. Drain. Cool. Let stand in sweetened vinegar (the same as for Vinegared Fresh Ginger). Add just a few drops of red food coloring, if desired.

Flowered Turnips
KIKKA KABU

5 small turnips
Vinegar Mixture:
   3 tablespoons vinegar
   1½ tablespoons sugar
   ½ teaspoon salt
1 dried red pepper, cut thinly crosswise
salt

Cut off stem of turnips. Thinly pare, then level off both ends. Place stem side down on cutting board, then place a pair of chopsticks on both sides of turnip. Slice thinly down to chopsticks as on page 23. Put turnips in small bowl, sprinkle with salt. Place a few dishes (smaller than bowl) on top of turnips for weight. Set aside.

When turnips have softened, wash. Wipe and place them in dry bowl. Pour Vinegar Mixture over turnips. Let stand for 2 hours.

To Serve:
Shake off excess liquid. Lightly spread sliced top. Put a slice of red pepper in center and garnish with chrysanthemum leaves for flowerlike effect, if desired.

Seasonings, Spices and Herbs

GOMA (Sesame Seeds)

There are two kinds of sesame seeds: black and white. Toast each time before using. These are used to sprinkle over food for garnishing. Also used, when ground, for *Goma-zu* Sauce.

KINOME (Young leaves of Japanese Pepper Tree)

The fragrance, the bright green color and pretty shape of the tiny leaves are very prized for garnishing. As *kinome* begin to bud in early spring, the Japanese (who are very sensitive to the seasons) feel the coming of spring when they see *kinome* added to their food.

The fragrance is quite different, but sometimes parsley or watercress may be substituted for *kinome* for coloring.

KONA-WASABI (Powdered Japanese Horseradish)

Fresh horseradish has more flavor, but powdered ones are much cheaper and convenient to keep on hand.

MIRIN (Sweet *Sake*)

Mirin gives food sweetness, glaze and also improves taste.

Mirin may be substituted with 1 tablespoon *sake* and 1 teaspoon sugar.

MISO (Japanese Bean Paste)

There are many different kinds of *miso*. Some are salty, some are sweet. *Hatcho-miso* is dark in color and has a wonderful flavor. White *miso* is sweet and is used for some salad dressings.

MSG

Monosodium glutamate.

SAKE (Rice Wine)

For cooking it is not necessary to have the best *sake*, although decidedly inferior quality should be avoided. *Sake* adds a decided zest to cooking. As the cooking progresses, the *sake* alcohol evaporates but the delicious flavor remains and mellows.

SANSHO

A tangy Japanese spice, available ground and in seeds.

SHICHIMI-TOGARASHI (Seven Pepper Spice)

This is a good spice for sprinkling over "*Udon*," "*Mizutaki*," etc. Because it loses its aroma quickly, buy in small quantities and store tightly covered.

SOY SAUCE

There are two kinds of soy sauce: dark and light. The dark one is used for general cookery. When you do not want to change the bright colors of vegetables, use light soy sauce. As light soy sauce changes in quality once opened, plan to use it up as soon as possible.

VINEGAR

There are two kinds of vinegar: distilled and synthetic. Synthetic vinegar has a stronger taste and less flavor than distilled brands. Use distilled vinegar to make good "*Sushi*" and "*Sunomono*."

YUZU (Lime-like Citrus Fruit)

The juice, grated rind, and peel give an added lift to dishes, as lemon does. Slices may be used for garnishing.

Ingredients

ABURA-AGE
Deep-fried Soybean Curd.

AONORI
Green seaweed.

BENI SHOGA
Red pickled ginger root, available bottled.

DAIKON (Giant White Radish)
These are used either raw or boiled. Turnips may be used as a substitue.

KAMABOKO (Boiled Fish Cake)
This is mostly white and shaped in a semi-circular mound on a small oblong board. It is used in "*Chawan-mushi*," and it is some-times eaten as a kind of side dish.

KAMPYO
Dried gourd shavings, available in packets.

KATAKURIKO
Corn-flour or cornstarch.

KIKURAGE
Cloud ears a cup-shaped mushroom with a spongy texture.

KONBU **OR** *KOMBU* (Dried Kelp)
Sometimes this is called *dashi-kombu*. It is used as a base for soup stock.

KOYA-DOFU (Dried Frozen Bean Curd)
This is used for boiled dishes.

MATSUTAKE
Large Japanese mushrooms, available canned.

MITSUBA (A Kind of Trefoil)
This is used in soup, "*Chawan-mushi*," etc., for color and fragrance. Watercress may sometimes be substituted for *mitsuba*.

NAMA-JIITAKE
Fresh *shiitake*.

NIBOSHI
Small dried fish, resembling young sardine.

NORI (Dried Sheets of Laver Seaweed)
This is used for "*Norimaki*," garnishing or relishes. Dry over low heat before using. Crumble or cut into thin strips. Store *nori* in air tight container in refrigerator to keep dry.

SHIITAKE
A large flat mushroom.

SHIRASUBOSHI
Dried small white fish.

SHIRATAKI (Root Starch Noodles)
These thin noodles are made from the roots of a certain Japanese plant called "*Konn-yaku*." It is used in "*Sukiyaki*" and "*Mizu-taki*."

SHUNGIKU (A Green Leafy Vegetable of the Crysanthemum Family)
Spinach may be substituted for *shungiku* in "*Sukiyaki*" and "*Mizutaki*." Mince for garnishing; or use snipped parsley as a substitute.

SOMEN (Vermicelli)
These are fine-shaped noodles used in soups.

TAMAGO-ZOMEN (Egg Noodles)
Plain *somen* noodles are white, but *tamago-zomen* have a light lemon color, as they have a small amount of egg yolk.

TOFU (Soybean Curd)
This is used in *Miso* Soups, "*Sukiyaki*," etc., and is high in protein.

UMEBOSHI
Pickled plums.

UDON (Wide Flat Noodles)
Both the dried variety and freshly boiled variety are sold. Spaghetti is thinner, but may be substituted for *udon*.

YAKI-FU
This is made of wheat gluten and is used in "*Sukiyaki*".

YAKI-DOFU
Roasted Soybean Curd.

WAKAME (A Kind of Dried Seaweed)
This is used in *Miso* Soups and Salads.

Index of Recipes